How to Publish on Kindle

Everything You Need to Know to get your
Book Published on Amazon Kindle

Richard G Lowe, Jr

How to Publish on Kindle

Everything You Need to Know to get your Book Published on Amazon Kindle

Publish Your Book Series #2

Published by The Writing King
www.thewritingking.com

How to Publish on Kindle

ASIN: B01LZUI61Y
ISBN: 978-1-943517-83-1 (Hardcover)
ISBN: 978-1-943517-82-4 (Paperback)
ISBN: 978-1-943517-43-5 (eBook)

Proofreading by Jilly Prather.

Table of Contents

Table of Contents

Introduction

Why have I written a book about publishing on the Kindle? Aren't there plenty of other books on the subject? Isn't the help within the KDP application sufficient?

My goal was to create a book which describes exactly, step-by-step, how to take a manuscript all the way through the process needed to publish on the Kindle, without any diversions. I've kept it simple and to-the-point, and also given notes on the various decisions you need to make throughout the process, and the ramifications of those decisions. By making the right choices at the beginning, you can make it easier later on down the road.

***

Once you've written a book, the next hurdle is figuring out how to publish it. These days, there are a vast number of options available for getting your book out to your audience — those people who want to read what you've written enough to spend their hard-earned money and time.

In the past, your options were much more limited. You could go to a publisher, usually via an agent, and convince them that your book would sell. Since books were printed in advance, and distributed to bookstores and libraries, a publisher had to be sure that there was a good market before taking a chance on your product. Otherwise, they could print a lot of paper that would sit in warehouses or be returned for destruction. In other words, they wanted to be sure they would make money before investing in your project.

Introduction

Your other option was to publish using a vanity press. This meant that you paid a company to print a certain number of copies of your book, anywhere from a few hundred to a few thousand. You'd receive all of them yourself, storing them in your garage or a storage unit, and then figure out how to market and sell them. Of course, the vanity press promised they would help you market, but somehow that never seemed to happen and royalties and riches were very rare under this model.

In the twenty-first century, the world of publishing has changed dramatically. A whole new paradigm called self-publishing has burst upon the world that has made it possible for anyone –regardless of social status, income, or anything else – to publish their book and sell it on major markets such as Amazon, Barnes & Noble or iBook. Now you can publish your book without worrying about whether or not it will make money – although, I'm sure, you'd prefer to get some income from your hard work.

Amazon turned the world upside down again by creating the Kindle, an inexpensive electronic library of books that people can carry around with them. Suddenly, anyone could purchase hundreds or even thousands of books and store them on a device the size of a paperback, reading them anywhere they wanted.

Naturally, there were alternatives to the Kindle both before and after it came onto the scene. However, Kindle offered something that other businesses couldn't: it was inexpensive and had access to Amazon's vast library of books and other materials.

The Kindle has become so popular that it has practically supplanted every other book reading device, with the possible exception of Apple tablets and the iBook marketplace.

The long and short of it is that if you self-publish a book, you would be well advised to ensure that it is available on the Kindle. It's a huge market, the royalties are significant, and publishing is relatively simple.

The purpose of this book is to describe the steps you need to accomplish in order to publish your manuscript on the Kindle. I will begin by describing the steps you should take before you log into your Kindle account, and continue through to the point where your book is live on Amazon.

There are a few caveats and best practices that I will describe, some that I learned the hard way and others that I picked up in various courses, forums and speaking to experts.

Important: the product KinSEO gives you vital information on how to optimize your books title, subtitle and description to get additional sales.

https://www.thewritingking.com/kinseo/

***

As of the writing of this book, I've published over thirty volumes on Kindle, and I've learned quite a bit about how to make the platform work properly. My purpose in writing this book for you is to pass along the information that I've learned in the hopes that you can take better advantage of KDP to get

Introduction

your book published properly so it will make you a good income.

I hope you enjoy what I've written and find it to be of some value. If you would like to send me a note about this book, feel free to write me at rich@thewritingking.com. If you enjoyed the book, please write a positive review.

Before you Publish

Before you can begin publishing your book on Kindle using Amazon's KDP website, there are a few things you need to have ready. Each of these items is described more fully in the following chapters and briefly identified here in this chapter.

A Book – Obviously, you need to have a manuscript ready to be published. This is a document in Microsoft Word format. KDP supports a number of other formats, but Word is by far the easiest for most people.

Book Cover – You book needs a graphic image to serve as a cover. This must contain your title and subtitle, as well as the author name. You should also include the name of the series, if applicable.

A Title – All books require a title which should contain keywords that are used to help people find your book on Amazon. Additionally, the title must be descriptive of what your book is about. Note that your title as entered into KDP must exactly match the title printed on your book cover.

Subtitle – This is a continuation of your title, and contains more information and keywords to help describe the contents of your book. You don't have to have a subtitle, but it does give you additional room to further describe what your manuscript is about to your readers and to provide additional search keywords.

Series – You can optionally include the name of the series to which your book belongs, as well as the number of that serious. For example, this book is 1st in the "Publish Your Book" series.

Edition – Optionally, you can specify the edition number of your book. This is useful if you had made major updates to the content and want to differentiate between the two versions.

Publisher – This is the name of the company or person publishing your book. If you are self-publishing, you can (and should) create your own publishing "company."

Description – The detailed information describing why your readers should purchase your book as well as information about the contents.

Book Contributors – A list of all of the people who helped with the book.

Language – What language is your book written in?

ISBN number – Paperback and hardcover books require ISBN numbers, but they are optional on electronic books such as on the Kindle. One of the advantages to including an ISBN number is that it makes it possible to sell your books to libraries.

Categories – Buyers can search for your book using pre-defined categories. Picking the right categories (you have two choices) is essential for good sales.

Search Keywords – A list of up to seven keywords which Amazon will use to help buyers find your book. Picking the right keywords is essential for sales, and those keywords should also appear in your title, subtitle, and description.

Price – Do some research on Amazon to figure out which price you want to set for your book. This determines not only what people will pay, but how much you'll make in royalties.

***

A note about book reviews

Book reviews may be associated with any one version of your book – paperback, hardcover, Kindle or Audiobook. Readers may write reviews on any version they wish. However, when asking for book reviews, try and get them on the Kindle version. The reason is you can easily change the title and other information on the Kindle, while you cannot change it on paperbacks. This means if you DO want to change the title of your paperback, you have to essentially delete it (unpublish it) and republish it – which losses all book reviews on the paperback version.

***

The following sections go through all of the information needed by the KDP application (website) more-or-less in the same order as they appear on the KDP website. The book manuscript and cover are discussed first because they are vital and must be prepared before you publish.

Each question asked by KDP is described in detail, along with the ramifications of possible answers.

Your Book

I think it should be obvious that the most important thing you have to complete before you can publish a book is a manuscript. The format of choice is a DOCX file created by Microsoft Word, although KDP supports several others, including HTML, MOBI, ePub, RTF, TXT, PDF, and KPE.

Once you upload your file to KDP it will be converted to MOBI format, which is what Kindle uses internally.

One thing to keep in mind as you are creating and formatting your manuscript is MOBI is designed to work on a wide variety of devices, not just a Kindle. In fact, you can download an application to run it on your desktop, smartphone, and even Apple Computer systems. Because of this, any graphics or other formatting that you do may not display the same on all devices.

MOBI is very restrictive about the type of formatting that you can perform in your manuscript. You cannot use bulleted or numbered lists. Unfortunately, if you do include them, no errors will be generated and the MOBI file will be created just fine. It will, however, not display properly on all devices.

When you want to use a bulleted list, you should create it manually as shown in the example below:

* list 1
* list 2
* list 3

Your Book

Yes, I know it sounds unbelievable that you have to do something so primitive, but that's the nature of the beast.

In fact, you can't use any fancy formatting at all – text boxes, sidebars, drop caps, placed text and images, embedded fonts, and so forth won't work on the Kindle.

You can include graphics, but keep in mind that due to the vast number of different devices that your document could be displayed upon, the graphics will not show exactly like you think they should.

The best thing to do with graphics is to place each one on its own line, centered. This will work on any device in both portrait and landscape mode. Any other positioning of graphics will disappoint you and your readers.

Use style for headers and other elements in your manuscript. This will make it easier to change if you decide you want more spaces, bolding or some other formatting.

If you are publishing a paperback version

In the instance where you are also publishing a paperback version, you will need to copy all of the contents of your Kindle version to a separate file for uploading to Createspace (or other publisher.) This is because you can specify much more detailed formatting for paperback – basically all of the formatting supported by Word.

For this reason, don't begin creating your paperback version until after all editing and proofreading are complete. Otherwise, you'll have to make corrections in both versions.

Another important difference between Kindle and Paperback is on Kindle, you can change every bit of data about the book at any time before or after publication. This includes the title, subtitle, series, manuscript, and cover.

Createspace will not allow you to change any metadata including the title, subtitle, series, author, ISBN number, edition and so forth after the book has been published. If, down the road, you want to change the title or any of this information, the only way to do it is to unpublish the book and create a new version with the new information. This results in the loss of any reviews associated with the old version.

A note about the Table of Contents

You can use the built-in Table of Contents feature of Microsoft Word to embed the contents into your manuscript, and that will work just fine on Kindle. However, to prepare your document for other publishing platforms such as Smashwords, you should create your table of contents manually using bookmarks and hyperlinks.

Smashwords, which is a publishing platform that allows you to publish your book on a wide variety of other publishers including iBook and Nook, does not support the Microsoft Word table of contents.

To do this manually, insert a bookmark at the start of each header you want to include in your table of contents. After that, manually enter each line in the table the contents and hyperlink each one to the appropriate bookmark.

Your Book

If you believe you are never going to publish on Smashwords, then there is no need to go through this trouble. However, doing so will prevent you from having to do the work later on.

Note that if you create an index or a table of figures, and you intend to publish on Smashwords, you must not use the built-in functions of Microsoft Word. Create them manually using bookmarks and hyperlinks.

Editing

Spend the time and effort to get your book professionally proofread and edited before you publish. This will ensure your book maintains a high level of quality.

No book is perfect, and a typo or grammar error inevitably occurs, even in books released by professional, high-end publishing houses. However, if you want to be taken seriously as an author, ensure your books have good grammar and spelling.

A professional editor will help you with plotting and character issues in fiction works, as well as with transitions between chapters, sections and even paragraphs. In fact, an editor will help you polish your book and ensure it reads well, supports your arguments or plot, and is complete.

Another option is to attend writing critique groups. A site such as meetup is excellent for finding one of these groups in your area. These are made up of writers who help each other find issues with their works. I've found these to be of immeasurable influence on my writing because they help me find issues that, alone, I would never have noticed.

The All-Important Cover

One of the most important factors in being able to make sales of your book is the quality of your cover. If your cover is not great, you aren't going to sell a lot of books — it's that simple.

But what differentiates a cover that will sell books from a cover that won't?

One of the best things you can do is take a look at the covers of books that have already been published in your categories and niche. Look at the top twenty books, those on the first page in the category, because those are the top sellers. This means these authors have created a product, including the cover, which is selling.

Look over those covers carefully, and note the positioning of all of the various elements. You'll see some common themes. There is usually a picture of some kind which may or may not have anything to do with what's inside the book. The purpose of the picture is not necessarily to describe the contents; rather, the picture is intended to entice the reader, to catch his or her attention long enough that they read the description and other information about the book.

Also, note the typefaces and fonts that are used on those covers. The font should be easy to read, clean, and appropriate to your book or genre.

Your title should be large enough that it can be read when the cover is viewed as a thumbnail. Remember, most people are going to be searching for your book, which means the cover will show in thumbnail form in the search listings. So it's important that they be able to read the title and the picture makes sense at that smaller size.

The other information needs to be readable, but is not as important. You definitely want to include your series, author, and subtitle but you can position them anywhere you want as long as they can be seen and read.

Covers are best when they are simple. A single picture or two that gets the message across is much better than a complex collection of a dozen images.

Be careful when using stock images, especially those available for free. This is because lots of authors use the same images, and you may find yourself with the book looks the same as everyone else's.

Ensure any images you use are either public domain, available via a free license such as Creative Commons, or have been legally purchased from a stock image site (or you created the images yourself.)

The art and science of creating a great cover is a subject for another whole book and even a course. Thus, I'm not going into it in any further detail here.

However, one thing you can do is join some writing groups, and use them to get opinions on your covers. Present several options and ask which is best. This can help you eliminate some terrible ones before they get into print.

Don't hesitate to change covers over time. You can change them out any time you want. If your book isn't selling, a poorly designed cover or one that simply doesn't resonate with your audience is often the reason. Changing a cover can result in an immediate improvement in sales.

The Title

Your title is one of the most important components of your book's metadata (the information about your book, as opposed to the information within your book.)

Obviously, your title communicates to your potential buyers and readers what kind of information or story is contained inside. Your title must communicate well to your readership so that they are enticed and want to purchase the book.

Additionally, Amazon depends on keywords and phrases contained in your title in order to build its index and help readers find your book. In fact, you'd be wise to place your primary keyword close to the front of your title, as Amazon gives that position extra weight.

Some authors will perform what is called keyword stuffing on their titles. It's always a good idea to include a few key phrases and words, however, you have to be careful that you aren't alienating your readers or creating convoluted titles that don't make sense.

Also, your entire title must be contained upon your cover and must exactly match what you enter into KDP. Thus, if you enter a 200 character long title, you may find it makes your cover crowded and unappealing.

You can't include any unauthorized references to other titles or authors and trademarked terms and you can't use a sales rank or a promotional statement such as "free".

The Title

Getting permission to use a trademarked term is not difficult. For example, let's say you were writing a book about LinkedIn. You want to include the word LinkedIn in your title, since that's what the book is about. LinkedIn, like many services on the web, has a page describing how their branded trademarks, logos, and graphics may be used by others. Review this document to find out how you can use those trademarks in your title. If you can't find that document, or it's unclear, send an email to the company.

When I was creating my book about LinkedIn, the rules described in their document were unclear to me. I wrote an email to the corporate office, and received a response a few days later which told me it was okay to use the word LinkedIn in the title of my book, as long the text was not large and was the same color and font as the rest of my title. They explained that this was so that it didn't appear that my book had been authorized by them. They also indicated that the LinkedIn logo could not ever be used on the front cover of any book.

Given that data, I was free to use the word LinkedIn on the cover, being careful to keep it the same size, font, and color as the rest of my title text.

Important note

One of the primary differences between books published in paperback and on Kindle is that the title, subtitle and other information about the book can be changed at any time for your Kindle version. However, you cannot change this information once you've published a paperback.

Thus, if you have a book with both the Kindle and paperback version, and you decide to change the title or subtitle of the Kindle copy, you'll have to leave the paperback unchanged (or publish the book, which loses all of its reviews, and republish a new version with the new title.)

If you do change the Kindle version of the book and not the paperback version (or the audiobook version if you have one) they will still remain linked on the same book page.

Subtitle

It's not essential to include a subtitle, but it does give you some extra space to be even more descriptive about your book and its contents. This can aid in helping buyers decide if they want to make a purchase.

The subtitle follows the same rules as the title, meaning you need to avoid using unauthorized trademarks, author names, and so on.

Additionally, keywords and phrases within the subtitle are used Amazon's index in order to make your book easier to find.

Series

If your book is part of a series, click the "This book is part of a series" checkbox.

Include the name of the series to which the book belongs. This ties them all together. For example, this book is the first volume within the "Publish Your Book" series, which contains a number of other books.

If you enter the series into KDP, you'll also need to enter the volume number within the series. It should be obvious, but you need to make the name of the series the same for every books in the series.

Keywords and phrases within the series are also used by Amazon for indexing purposes, although this is not as important as those in your title and description.

One of the reasons why including books in a series is a great idea is that customers often purchase other books within the same series. By intelligently grouping books in this manner, you can increase your sales, and you can market the whole series of books in addition to individual titles.

Edition Number

The addition number helps differentiate between revisions of your book. Let's say you created a book about sewing, then published it on Kindle. That would be your first edition.

Later, if you revise that book, and you want your readers to know that it's been changed, you can publish a new version as the second edition (or the third or the fourth as appropriate.)

It's important to note that you can make changes to the manuscript of your Kindle version, no matter how severe, at any point, and re-upload to update what's there. You are not required to create a new edition when you do this (this is true of both the paperback and the Kindle version.)

Thus, the edition is used only when you want to sell a new version of the book, generally if the information has been updated or changed in a major way.

This also allows you to keep the old edition on sale if desired, since each edition is a separate Kindle publication.

Publisher

If you are self-publishing, you should define your own publisher. Not using one means the publisher will be Amazon Digital Services.

For example, at the time of this writing I have self-published thirty-five books. To brand them all as my books, I created a publishing company called The Writing King₸ and purchased a block of ISBN numbers associated with that publisher.

Entering the name of a publisher is optional, but it's advantageous to group all of your own works together under a common umbrella.

This can be either your name or the name of your publishing company. The publisher's name is included on the book detail page on Amazon.

You can't use the name of another publishing company, even if they published a previous edition of your book. You also can't reference Amazon, Kindle, KDP, websites or domain names.

Creating a publishing company and publishing your own books under that name increases the credibility of your brand. Additionally, many libraries don't accept self-published books (although this statement applies more to paperbacks than electronic books), but including the name of a publisher here makes it appear that the book has been professionally published.

Publisher

You can reinforce this by creating a blog or website that lists all of the books you published and other information. That gives your customers, librarians and bookstores a place to go to find all of your books outside of Amazon. The advantage of this is that you can include other places where the book has been published on your own blog or website.

Important Note

Even though this is often referred to as a Publishing Company, you do not need to actually define a real, legal company. This is just a name, yours or a fictitious one, that you use to publish your books.

Description

When a buyer visits your Amazon book page, the first thing they see is the title and subtitle, the cover, and the description. Based upon these elements, plus, to a lesser extent, the "look inside" feature, a person will make a decision as to whether or not to buy your book.

The quality of your description can mean the difference between your book selling well and not selling it all.

The first line of your description should include, preferably near the beginning, your primary keyword or phrase. The purpose of that first line is to grab your reader and pull him into your book.

The rest of the description serves the purpose of pushing the emotional buttons to get your reader to be interested in buying. Generally, you'll find you'll get more sales if you work on emotion rather than intellect.

People purchase based on fear, terror, anger, anxiety, and on the other side of the coin happiness, aesthetics, joy and so forth.

For example, if you want to sell a book about making money, the best way to do that is to work on greed and fear. You can also work on higher values such as a desire to make more money, feed one's family, go on a vacation and so forth. Mixing all these concepts together the description would work great.

Description

An excellent product called Hypnotic Book Descriptions goes into great detail about how to make a description that actually sells books.

https://www.thewritingking.com/hypnotic-book-descriptions/

Book Contributors

List anyone who contributed to the creation of your book. Obviously, this includes the author, but you can also list your editors, illustrators, narrators, photographers, and translators plus the people who wrote the forward, the introduction, and the preface.

First of all, it's just good manners to list those people who contributed to your book. Regardless of whether or not you hired them to perform the task, they put in the effort, and giving people credit helps them with their careers and portfolios.

In addition, every person that you list here is included in Amazon's index, which means that your book will come up on searches done on those people.

This can be especially valuable if you get a forward written by a famous person or influencer. Any searches done on the name of that influencer will also turn up your book, and this can increase your sales.

Languages

You can write and publish your book in a wide variety of languages. Amazon uses the language you select to sell your book on the appropriate country site.

If you want your book to be available in a number of other languages, you can use the Babelcube site to find and engage translators. You can also find your own translators and hire them to do the work for you.

Note if you use Babelcube, they submit the translated book to Amazon for you.

ISBN Number

You don't need an ISBN number to publish a book on Kindle. Amazon identifies all of its products, including books, by an ASIN number.

If you're on a budget and don't feel like spending the money, don't bother getting an ISBN number. You can sell your book just fine without it.

That being said, obtaining an ISBN number for your book has several distinct advantages.

First and foremost, it lists your book under the name of a publisher, whatever name you choose, as opposed to "Kindle Direct Publishing". If you're trying to brand yourself as a professional author, then it's best to separate yourself from the pack by including a publisher of your own.

This means you need to purchase a block of ISBN numbers from Bowker, which will cost you several hundred dollars. The best value is the 100-pack.

The same consideration applies whether you publish through Amazon or anywhere else. If you publish under a retailer, and don't have your own ISBN number, then your book will show the retailer as the publishing company. This indicates that your book has been self-published and implies that it is not professionally done.

Another reason to get your own ISBN number is Bowker (the repository of all ISBN numbers) maintains a Books In Print

ISBN Number

database which is submitted to search engines such as Google. If you want your ebook to appear in Google, it's best to get your own ISBN number. Doing so can get you additional sales from people searching on Google.

Verifying Your Publishing Rights

At this point, you need to verify that you have the right to publish everything in your book.

This includes not only your manuscript, but everything else including pictures, illustrations, large amounts of text and so on.

You must either own the copyrights on everything in your book, or have the permission of the copyright owner in order to include it.

You can use public domain materials within your book. For example, many old photographs and illustrations are available to anyone without charge, and you may feel free to use them.

On the other hand, trying to publish, unchanged, a copy of *20,000 Leagues Under the Sea* by Jules Vern would not be allowed by Amazon, because it doesn't add any value. However, if you took that same text and added some original pictures or commentary around it, then you can feel free to publish it.

US copyright law under the fair use rules allows you to use short passages from other works under certain conditions. For example, if you are writing a review column and reviewed a movie, you could include a short clip from the movie or a quote from one of the main characters. You can do this even though the movie is fully protected under copyright law.

Verifying Your Publishing Rights

There is a limit to fair use, however, and that you're not allowed to copy large amounts of text, say a whole page or five minutes from a movie, because that goes beyond the intent of fair use.

Categories

If you want your book to sell, it's important to choose the right categories, and to get your book to the "top" as quickly as possible. Categories are simply organized lists of books, with the bestselling (presumably the most popular) at the top. The order of books changes regularly, often hourly, based upon sales and other criteria. In general, the better your book is selling now the higher it will appear in the category. The algorithm used by Amazon is actually more complex, but this explanation will work for our discussion.

As a general rule of thumb, choosing the wrong category can be the kiss of death for book sales, while choosing the correct one can result in a bestseller.

I've found in talking with authors that one of the most difficult concepts is that of categories. Simply put, a category is a way to organize books on Amazon (and in libraries and bookstores) so they can be found.

Consider the example of a bookstore. Let's say each aisle is a different major subject – for example, Business Books.

Now, each bookcase within that aisle is another subject, so let's say this book is about Management.

Each shelf in the bookcase breaks down that subject even more. For example, our book about Management might be stored on the shelf containing Training.

Categories

So if you wanted to find a book about Management training, you'd start from the aisle called Business Books, find the bookcase titled Management, then find the self with the label Training.

Given this information, you might think it's a simple matter to find your category (Amazon allows you to enter 2 of them) and select the one you want.

Unfortunately, it is far more complicated than it might seem.

For a simple example, I chose the following categories under the KDP:

BUSINESS & ECONOMICS > Careers > Job Hunting
BUSINESS & ECONOMICS > Motivational

On my book page, this translates to:

Business & Money > Business Life > Etiquette
Business & Money > Job Hunting & Careers > Job Hunting
Business & Money > Management & Leadership > Motivational

Note that Amazon automatically added a third category.

That's a simple example. Unfortunately, there are many categories you cannot just add using the interface.

Some categories require that you include specific keywords under the "keywords" field of KDP.

For example, to put my book in the category:

Business & Money > Entrepreneurship & Small Business > Startups

I would need to include one of these keywords in the keyword field.

startup, startups

This is because there is no selection for "startups."

You can find out all about these special categories on this Amazon help page:

https://kdp.amazon.com/help?topicId=A200PDGPEIQX41

Sometimes I've found it is nearly impossible to figure out how to add my book to a specific category. The easiest thing to do in this case is email KDP support with your request. They will be happy to put your book into whatever category you desire, or tell you why it cannot be done.

Finally, don't be afraid to change your categories. If they are not working for you, by all means, change them. You may find your book performs better after your changes. If not, then change it again.

Age Range

If your book is intended for children, then set the age values as appropriate.

They are described on this Amazon help page:

https://kdp.amazon.com/help?topicId=AF9XK4TA1PSBV

If you set your age range to 18+, then you will not be able to change it later. Even KDP technical support will not make this change for you.

Setting this value for children and young adults will make it index appropriately on Amazon, making the book easier to find for your audience.

US Grade Range

The US Grade range is similar to the Age Range, and both should be set accordingly. This is just another way to narrow down the intended audience by age.

Keywords

Keywords help you book get discovered on Amazon. Correctly defining keywords can help your book get found, which will improve your sales. If you don't define your keywords properly, you will lose sales.

Finding the right keywords can be a major task. You can use tools such as Google Keyword Planner and Bing Keyword Research Tool to help. You can also use the search bar in Amazon to research keywords, and by looking at other books in your category, you may be able to ferret out a few from their description.

The subject of finding the right keywords (you are allowed seven of them) could take up a whole book in its own right, and will only be discussed briefly in this volume.

For the purposes of this discussion, let's say you have a business book about Management and Supervision. You might think you want to include the keywords "Management" and "Supervision." However, this would probably be a mistake.

The problem is everyone is using those keywords, so your book will be at the bottom of a long list of other books.

Instead, choose a more specific keyword or phrase. Instead of management or supervision, you might choose "my supervisor is harassing me" or "how to get promoted" or something along those lines. There will be far fewer books

Keywords

with these keywords, giving you a better chance to be at the top of the list.

Once you find the right keywords, use them in your title, subtitle, and description as described in KinSEO.

https://www.thewritingking.com/kinseo/

Do not hesitate to change your keywords often. If your book is not selling, changing your keywords can help.

Also, if you publish a paperback version and ensure it is linked to your book page (usually this is automatic) you will gain an additional five keywords. A good strategy is to make the keywords for your paperback be different than those for your Kindle version.

Upload or Create a Cover

We've already discussed the importance of book covers. At this point in the KDP screen, you'll need to actually upload it. If you don't upload a cover, Amazon will create a placeholder for you (this will probably reduce your sales to zero.)

You can read about KDP's cover requirements here:

https://kdp.amazon.com/help?topicId=A2J0TRG6OPX0VM

KDP may reject your cover for various reasons, but the error messages are pretty clear. Just correct the errors and upload it again.

Note you can change your book's cover at any time. In fact, if your book is not selling well, an excellent place to start is by changing the cover (after you change the keywords, title, and categories.)

Upload your Book File

This is the point where you send your book file to KDP. Just click the button and find it on your computer. It will take a few minutes to upload, then it will be converted to MOBI format while you watch. This usually doesn't take long, even for a large book.

Various errors can occur at this point, and you may need to resubmit your book more than once.

You can reupload you book at any time, including after it has been published.

Once your file has been uploaded, it will be checked for spelling. Any errors found will be displayed and you will have the option of ignoring them or continuing. If there are spelling errors, you will need to correct them in the manuscript and reupload.

Due to the extreme number of low quality books that have been published on KDP in the past, Amazon is policing spelling errors within books, and if too many are found the book could be suppressed (not listed) at the Amazon's discretion.

Preview Your Book

The moment of truth has arrived. You've defined everything about your book, uploaded your cover and given KDP your manuscript. There are no errors, so now it is time to check it out and see how it looks.

You have the option of reviewing you book online using the Online Previewer or downloading the MOBI version to your computer to look at on your own system. Amazon provides a previewer for both Mac and Windows for this purpose.

Regardless of which method you use, it's a good idea to scan through your book from the cover to the last page. It's much better to find and correct errors before publication than afterward.

If you do find errors, you'll need to correct them in the original manuscript and reupload.

Once you've finished reviewing your book and believe it's correct, it's time to move to the next page of KDP.

Verifying Your Publishing Territories

At this point, you can indicate you want to publish your book throughout the world, or just in specific countries and territories. If you want to limit it to specific locales, check the box next to each one. This could be useful to limit a certain translation to a specific country, or to exclude countries where you cannot publish for legal or other reasons.

Set Your Pricing and Royalty

It's time to enter how much you want to charge for your book. You can click the "View Service" button to ask Amazon to give you a report on what others have charged and recommend a good price for you.

Now select your royalty option: 35% or 70%. If your book is marked less than $2.99, you must select 35%.

If you select 70%, then you will be charged a small amount to deliver the book to the Kindle of the buyer. For books with just text and a few graphics, this is a minor charge. However, with heavy graphics, you may want to choose the 35% royalty rate.

The 35% royalty is useful if your book has a lot of graphics, making it very large. In this case, the delivery charge doesn't apply.

Set your prices for the various countries for your book. Note that normally, if the checkboxes are clicked, all country prices will be based upon your US price. You can see the estimated delivery costs and royalties for each country.

Kindle Matchbook

If you have produced a paperback version, you can click this box to give buyers a reduced price on the Kindle version. The royalties from this option will be the same as what you selected in the step above.

Kindle Book Lending

If you want to allow your book to be lent, check this box. The lending period is 14 days.

Confirm and Publish

Last, but not least, click the box saying you agree to all the terms and select "Save and Publish." A few hours (no more than 24 in general) your book will be live on Amazon.

Conclusions

You can literally publish as many books as you want in today's world of self-publishing. Platforms such as KDP for Kindle and Createspace for paperbacks have made it trivial to make your manuscripts available for sale on Amazon.

For virtually any book, it is essential that you get it out on the Kindle if you want to maximize your income. This is because Kindle sales make up a good amount of the total sales of books in the world. Not taking advantage of this platform is throwing money away.

Publishing a book on Kindle can be aggravating. The platform is simple enough, considering that you're actually creating a book, but there are caveats to virtually all of the information entered.

For example, categories and keywords must be correctly chosen in order for you to maximize your income. If you choose incorrectly, you may find that your book is not making any sales at all. On the other hand, chosen properly, categories and keywords can ensure your book sells even without promotion.

In this book, I've tried to document as many of the gotchas and not so obvious features that you can take advantage of or need to know in order to get your book to your audience.

Before you go

If you scroll to the last page in this eBook, you will have the opportunity to leave feedback and share the book with Before You Go. I'd be grateful if you turned to the last page and shared the book.

Also, if you have time, please leave a review. Positive reviews are incredibly useful. If you didn't like the book, please email me at rich@thewritingking.com and I'd be happy to get your input.

linkedin.thewritingking.com

About the Author

https://www.linkedin.com/in/richardlowejr
Feel free to send a connection request

Follow me on Twitter: @richardlowejr

Richard Lowe has leveraged more than 35 years of experience as a Senior Computer Manager and Designer at four companies into that of a bestselling author, blogger, ghostwriter, and public speaker. He has written hundreds of articles for blogs and ghostwritten more than a dozen books and has published manuscripts about computers, the Internet, surviving disasters, management, and human rights. He is currently working on a ten-volume science fiction series – the Peacekeeper Series – to be published at the rate of three volumes per year, beginning in 2016.

Richard started in the field of Information Technology, first as the Vice President of Consulting at Software Techniques, Inc. Because he craved action, after six years he moved on to work for two companies at the same time: he was the Vice President of Consulting at Beck Computer Systems and the Senior Designer at BIF Accutel. In January 1994, Richard found a home at Trader Joe's as the Director of Technical Services and Computer Operations. He remained with that incredible company for almost 20 years before taking an early retirement to begin a new life as a professional writer. He is currently the CEO of The Writing King, a company that provides all forms of writing services, the owner of The EBay King, and a Senior Branding Expert for LinkedIn Makeover. You can find a current list of all books on his Author Page and

About the Author

take a look at his exclusive line of coloring books at The Coloring King.

Richard has a quirky sense of humor and has found that life is full of joy and wonder. As he puts it, "This little ball of rock, mud, and water we call Earth is an incredible place, with many secrets to discover. Beings fill our corner of the universe, and some are happy, and others are sad, but each has their unique story to tell."

His philosophy is to take life with a light heart, and he approaches each day as a new source of happiness. Evil is ignored, discarded, or defeated; good is helped, enriched, and fulfilled. One of his primary interests is to educate people about their <u>human rights</u> and assist them to learn how to be <u>happy in life</u>.

Richard spent many <u>happy days</u> hiking in national parks, crawling over boulders, and peering at Indian pictographs. He toured the Channel Islands off Santa Barbara and stared in fascination at wasps building their homes in Anza-Borrego. One of his joys is <u>photography</u>, and he has photographed more than 1,200 belly dancing events, as well as dozens of Renaissance fairs all over the country.

Because writing is his passion, Richard remains incredibly creative and prolific; each day he writes between 5,000 and 10,000 words, diligently using language to bring life to the world so that others may learn and be entertained.

Richard is the CEO of The Writing King, which specializes in fulfilling any writing need. You can find out more at <u>https://www.thewritingking.com/</u>, and emails are welcome at <u>rich@thewritingking.com</u>

Books by Richard G Lowe Jr.

Business Professional Series

On the Professional Code of Ethics and Business Conduct in the Workplace – Professional Ethics: 100 Tips to Improve Your Professional Life - have you ever wondered what it takes to be successful in the professional world? This book gives you some tips that will improve your job and your career.

Help! My Boss is Whacko! - How to Deal with a Hostile Work Environment - sometimes the problem is the boss. There are all kinds of managers, some competent, some incompetent, and others just plain whacked. This book will help you understand and handle those different types of managers.

Help! I've Lost My Job: Tips on What to do When You're Unexpectedly Unemployed – suddenly having to leave your job can be a harsh and emotional time in your life. Learn some of the things that you need to consider and handle if this happens to you.

Help! My Job Sucks Insider Tips on Making Your Job More Satisfying and Improving Your Career – sometimes conditions conspire to make the regular trek to a job feel like a trip through Dante's Inferno. Sometimes, these are out of our control, such as a malicious manager or incompetent colleague. On the other hand, we can take control of our lives and workplace and improve our situation. Get this book to learn what you can do when your job sucks.

Books by Richard G Lowe Jr.

How to Manage a Consulting Project: Make money, get your project done on time, and get referred again and again – I found that being a consultant is a great way to earn a living. Managing a consulting project can be a challenge. This book contains some tips to help you so you can deliver a better product or service to your customers.

How to be a Good Manager and Supervisor, and How to Delegate – Lessons Learned from the Trenches: Insider Secrets for Managers and Supervisors – I've been a manager for over thirty years I learned many things about how to get the job done and deliver quality service. The information in this book will help you manage your projects to a high level of quality.

Focus on LinkedIn – Learn how to create a LinkedIn profile and to network effectively using the #1 business social media site.

Home Computer Security Series

Safe Computing is Like Safe Sex: You have to practice it to avoid infection – Security expert and Computer Executive, Richard Lowe, presents the simple steps you can take to protect your computer, photos and information from evil doers and viruses. Using easy-to-understand examples and simple explanations, Lowe explains why hackers want your system, what they do with your information, and what you can do to keep them at bay. Lowe answers the question: how to you keep yourself say in the wild west of the internet.

Books by Richard G Lowe Jr.

Disaster Preparation and Survival Series

Real World Survival Tips and Survival Guide: Preparing for and Surviving Disasters with Survival Skills – CERT (Civilian Emergency Response Team) trained and Disaster Recovery Specialist, Richard Lowe, lays out how to make you, your family, and your friends ready for any disaster, large or small. Based upon specialized training, interviews with experts and personal experience, Lowe answers the big question: what is the secret to improving the odds of survival even after a big disaster?

Creating a Bug Out Bag to Save Your Life: What you need to pack for emergency evacuations - When you are ordered to evacuate—or leave of your free will—you probably won't have a lot of time to gather your belongings and the things you'll need. You may have just a few minutes to get out of your home. The best preparation for evacuation is to create what is called a bug out bag. These are also known as go-bags, as in, "grab it and go!"

Professional Freelance Writer Series

How to Operate a Freelance Writing Business, and How to be a Ghostwriter – Proven Tips and Tricks Every Author Needs to Know about Freelance Writing: Insider Secrets from a Professional Ghostwriter – This book explains how to be a ghostwriter, and gives tips on everything from finding customers to creating a statement of work to delivering your final product.

How to Write a Blog That Sells and How to Make Money From Blogging: Insider Secrets from a Professional Blogger:

Books by Richard G Lowe Jr.

<u>Proven Tips and Tricks Every Blogger Needs to Know to Make Money</u> – There is an art to writing an article that prompts the reader to make a decision to do something. That's the narrow focus of this book. You will learn how to create an article that gets a reader interested, entices them, informs them, and causes them to make a decision when they reach the end.

Other Books by Richard Lowe Jr

How to Be Friends with Women: How to Surround Yourself with Beautiful Women without Being Sleazy – I am a photographer and frequently find myself surrounded by some of the most beautiful women in the world. This book explains how men can attract women and keep them as friends, which can often lead to real, fulfilling relationships.

How to Throw Parties like a Professional: Tips to Help You Succeed with Putting on a Party Event – Many of us have put on parties, and I know it can be a daunting and confusing experience. In this book, I share what I learned from hosting small house parties to shows and events.

Additional Resources

Is your career important to you? Find out how to move your career in any direction you desire, improve your long-term livelihood, and be prepared for any eventuality. Visit the page below to sign up to receive valuable tips via email, and to get a free eBook about how to optimize your LinkedIn profile.

http://list.thewritingking.com/

I've written and published many books on a variety of subjects. They are all listed on the following page.

https://www.thewritingking.com/books/

On that site, I also publish articles about business, writing, and other subjects. You can visit by clicking the following link:

https://www.thewritingking.com

To find out more about me or my photography, you can visit these sites:

Personal website: https://www.richardlowe.com
Photography: http://www.richardlowejr.com
LinkedIn Profile: https://www.linkedin.com/in/richardlowejr
Twitter: https://twitter.com/richardlowejr

If you have any comments about this book, feel free to email me at rich@thewritingking.com

Premium Writing Services

Do you have a story that needs to be told? Have you been trying to write a book for ages but never can seem to find the time to get it done? Do you want to brand your business, but don't know how to get started?

The Writing King has the answer. We can help you with any of your writing needs.

Ghostwriting. We can write your book, which entails interviewing you to get your story, writing the book and then working with you to revise it until complete. To discuss your book, contact The Writing King today.

Website Copy. Many businesses include the text on their sites as an afterthought, and that can result in lost sales and leads. Hire The Writing King to review your site and recommend changes to the text which will help communicate your message and improve your sales.

Blogging. Build engagement with your customers by hiring us to write a weekly or semi-weekly article for your blog, LinkedIn or other social media. Contact The Writing King today to discuss your blogging needs.

LinkedIn. LinkedIn is of the most important vehicles for finding new business, and a professionally written profile works to pulling in those leads. Write or update your profile today.

Technical Writing. We have broad experience in the computer, warehousing and retail industries, and have

Premium Writing Services

written hundreds of technical documents. Contact The Writing King today to find out how we can help you with your technical writing project.

The Writing King has the skills and knowledge to help you with any of your writing needs. Call us today to discuss how we can help you.

www.ingramcontent.com/pod-product-compliance
Lightning Source LLC
Chambersburg PA
CBHW071509210326
41597CB00018B/2709